praise for tend

"These poems are an elegant romp through tangled city gardens and teeming waste bins of memory and human consciousness. The domestic realm is a wilderness, a trash heap, a broken string of pearls. All at once this beautiful book is the milky crystal on the green chain, the broken eggshell in your compost, the lost slipper through a rotten board. *tend* takes your hand."
—Shannon Bramer, author of *Precious Energy*

"*tend* is a master class in poetic restraint. Hargreaves' brilliance lies in her ability to cleave poems to their core, to 'strip words/like veins from a leg/or bones from a fish.' She is ruthless in her delivery— stacks lines together like kindling for a fire, drops a lit match and walks away, leaving the reader to smoulder."
—Adrienne Gruber, author of *Q & A*

"Clever and controlled, *tend* grounds you in the gross and astounding musculature of language, and doesn't skimp on the viscera. The poems in this collection gather and sing to the ways in which we tend to ourselves, to the world, and to others—and how so often these messy, generous acts bleed together. Through rituals, commands, instructions, and advice, Hargreaves expertly engages a variety of tactics and wields a distinct yet collective lyrical voice with a scalpel-like precision. I felt like I lived in the body of every poem, and every poem lived in the specific, chaotic detritus of the world."
—Domenica Martinello, author of *All Day I Dream About Sirens*

"*tend* is an apiary of lists buzzing with to-dos that lilt and tilt. Hargreaves skillfully merges a miscellany of terms and quicksilver minutes into a work of persistence. Day to day knickknacks slip next to gentle warnings and medical debris. A work full of mettle."
—Christine McNair, author of *Charm* and *Conflict*

T0036515

praise for Leak

"*Leak* is an exciting poetic debut which performs a relentless and passionate anatomy through syntax that spills, kicks, craves, bloats, sheds, and spits. Hargreaves reminds us that, for worse and for better, parts of speech and speaker tend to gurgle beyond their notional grammars. Read it and gush."
—Susan Holbrook

"With deliberate caprice, Kate Hargreaves executes, deranges, disentangles, fractures, accidenting language into dazzling constellations."
—Rosemary Nixon

"A *tour de aperture*, these poems will leak from your tongue into your brain, gushing pleasure: pleasure: pleasure: pleasure."
—Nicole Markotić

"The collection is best read aloud, the tongue tripping over Hargreaves's delightful lyrical trickery. With each play on words, her love of language is evident, right down to each descriptive stanza."
—*Room Magazine*

"*Leak* is striking for the sounds Hargreaves generates, allowing the language to roll and toss and spin in a fantastic display of gymnastic aural play so strong one can't help but hear the words leap off the page."
—rob mclennan

tend

Book*hug Press
Toronto 2022

tend

poems · Kate Hargreaves

Library and Archives Canada Cataloguing in Publication
Title: Tend / Kate Hargreaves.
Names: Hargreaves, Kate, author.
Description: Poems.
Identifiers: Canadiana (print) 20220210292 | Canadiana (ebook)
20220210446
   ISBN 9781771667814 (softcover)
   ISBN 9781771667838 (PDF)
   ISBN 9781771667821 (EPUB)
Classification: LCC PS8615.A727 T46 2022 | DDC C811/.6—dc23

The production of this book was made possible through the
generous assistance of the Canada Council for the Arts and the
Ontario Arts Council. Book*hug Press also acknowledges the
support of the Government of Canada through the Canada Book
Fund and the Government of Ontario through the Ontario Book
Publishing Tax Credit and the Ontario Book Fund.

Book*hug Press acknowledges that the land on which we operate is
the traditional territory of many nations, including the Mississaugas
of the Credit, the Anishnabeg, the Chippewa, the Haudenosaunee,
and the Wendat peoples. We recognize the enduring presence of
many diverse First Nations, Inuit, and Métis peoples and are grateful
for the opportunity to meet, work, and learn on this territory.

Book*hug Press

for O, finally

contents

i

unsolicited

the young ones

we are the young ones
and we have come for your sons
our pants stretch tight over thighs and button high
we mix patterns and clash colours
shun linen for synthetic blends
we have undercut sections of our collective hair
crisped with heat and bleach
our shoes are plastic and worn through at the toes
we choose wines for their labels
eat processed cheese
hold paring knives at awkward angles
and have never once used a mortar and pestle
we can't say we've made it to Provence
but we got wasted in Québec at eighteen
we pepper our speech with fucking
and are, like, inarticulate
our acne scars gleam under highlighter
our toenails are black
and we make public shows of weeping
give us their hands and we'll lead them
              through sweat-stained crowds
or into woods toward artificial lakes
away from sleepy houses, downtown to the river
we'll twirl and show our teeth until the sun creeps up
spill shawarma sauce down our necks
smear it with the backs of our hands
disappear into duplexes and cheap upholstery
we will call the next evening, and they will listen
stuff their ears with cotton against pleas to stay
feel the drag toward our caffeine habits
the way we run, glancing back over shoulders
our distaste for names and datebooks and chairs
they will bang on our doors and shout toward our windows
denounce addresses and object permanence
press us to emerge again and lead them

to burn popcorn for dinner
cut hair with nail scissors
relinquish IDs to sticky tables
skin knees stumbling on sidewalks
tail cats through unlocked gates
        and wind-buckled screen doors
we have come for your sons
to wash away their potential
we cannot garden
we do not try
but oh, how we laugh

plans

I'm leaving town to felt shirts out of belly button lint
got big plans for the coast
    where snow doesn't harden
    and you can leave keys in your door
    making proposals to salt water
I'll learn to weave long underwear
    out of barbershop trimmings
melt acrylic nails down for windowpanes
and pulp utility bills into letter stock

I've been collecting eggshells to grind into pills
    to reset my bones and fix my legs to the soil
drawing ink from avocado pits
and lining sills with water glasses
    tying my shoelaces to bike racks
    so I don't wander back east

I'll commit to the coast
    to polish my toes in the sand
        and tumble shards and nails into gems
        wrap the remnants in gold wire
    layer scarves in the winter
    and mail the dust back home

an early gift for February 14

T

an acoustic shadow the shape of
echogenic arms
medical-grade plastic

     loose and   wandering
white cross *just bigger than a toonie*

     floats in a world of pink and pinker
and fluid red

     and.

The x-ray tech shoots film of my insides
says I can pay five dollars to download the snaps
     from home.
save them to my "personal PC" to respond to
requests to *sendnudes.*

Lower torso minus clothes,
minus skin minus organs.

Just bones bones and a ·
     white   T
Autoreply to a dick pic.

A rogue letter bumps against bladder walls
digs pink divots
     pinker.

Silvers   a   snail trail of
     proges t erone   behind.

     Proges t in

Levonorges t rel

Loveges t eronal

Love   jester   own   all

softer le tt ers
        in a friendly pink pamphlet
        stock photo mother
        sharp single
        T

dug its way through my uterus last Monday,
wiggled through walls and poked out the other side,
an earring pushed through a years-sealed hole.

        T

Rattled my insides until I folded into
t   wo

tilt ed

the in-training tech pressed
        bladder kicking harder

stack your fists behind your back

twenty-three minutes of
polite bracing shaking legs

they'll call with results and GPS coordinates
longitude/latitude of lost letters
        slipping behind my bowel

t il t
clamps pry pinheads into straw widths
splitting the space behind belly button
a butter knife under fingernails

two
inches
deep

They'll need special tools to remove it
tongs and sounds grasping at invisible strings
We'll just yank it (out turn you inside
borders of your body
aren't

guts and medical-grade plastic

        T

        T
swea t   spli   tt   ing exam paper

T
        t   ickling linoleum

thank yourself for this practice

push a little juiciness into your shoulders
relax your toenails
and sink your eyelashes into their roots
wiggle your shins like you were a ladybird
and press your collarbones firmly into the foundations
of the building
spread your toes shoulder-width as best you can
arch your forehead
wriggle your lips
and relax every little hair in your nose
as if they'd had a couple glasses of a strong sangria
pull your teeth into your chest
letting go of any panic when you
open your knees wide and
backhand the person to your right
roll up up up one follicle at a time
and pause here
cultivating the blood in your ears
ankles swelling
take inventory of your itchy cheek
and if you must move *decide* to scratch
pool your cracking bones
let go of your bowels
the roll escaping your exercise pants
the zipper boring through your lower back
the shifting thong
the snot crusting in one nostril
and fluttering with each breath
the sleep gunk gluing together your eyelids
the sock fuzz under your baby toenail
the hairs pushing through the skin of your armpits
take stock in this moment
of the fluid in your ears
the curve in your back
the weight of your scars

unsolicited

I don't know who needs to hear this, but
—those scabs are starting to weep.

I don't know who needs to hear this, but
—knock twice when tempted to scratch.

I don't know who needs to hear this, but
—dehisce is not a sound.
—elevate the heart.
—chew magnesium for cramps.

I don't know who needs to read this, but
—no one's hitting ten thousand steps.

I don't know who needs to test this, but
—the higher, the closer to god.

I don't know who needs to feel this, but
—I don't know who needs to know this, but

I don't know what else to tell you, but
—your hold time is forty-two minutes.

I don't know who heeds a warning, but
—don't shower or eat after midnight.

I don't know if you missed the memo, but
—sick days just aren't in your contract.

I know it might be a stretch, but
—hold corpse pose and beg for relief.

I don't know who's already numb, but
—pinch twice before digging in.

I don't know who finds themselves splitting, but

I don't know whose edges are fraying, but

I don't know your threshold for asking, but
—a cobbler can patch up those seams.

ii

pattern

rerun

wild horses can't make matter-of-fact my hand in your pocket scarf
over face thinking you must be quoting the Sundays version and
not the original since we heard it while making dinner from the
living-room tv last night on the credits of that one episode where
she finally gets the guy to dance and then he leaves—it's just that I
don't have much time writing out Spanish flash cards and adding
cartoon birds to the margins, but soon it'll be *just poems*, not a book
or anything, *just nouns*:

plum

                      centipede

      desk lamp

                  muskrat

                                    tea kettle

                trousers

pattern

Chain (ch) 8. Single crochet (sc) in each of 7 chs except first. Turn.
Ch 1. Sc 1. Double crochet (reverse) next 2 scs.
Turn.

Chain 4. Single single 2(gether). Double-double with half-and-half.
Apple turn(over).

Decrease space over next 4 wks. Turn 1 clock back. Reverse.
Unravel 5 rows and change.

Turnaround, loop back. Beg together (tog) again. Sk ahead to third
date. Cut off loose ends.

Sl off. Reduce space. Double2tog in F(our)P(oster).
reptog.
reptog.

Sk single hookups. 1 st in time sv (save) 9.

Cont tog for next 2 months. Wrap round little finger. Slip 1 ring. Yo
(yarn over) eyes. Toss and turn.

7 rounds at the Loop. Inc tension. 4 rows. Sk town, reverse, and beg
again single. Your round.

other people's dogs

i.

the   buzz
of wanting
your
            photo of the dog with a goofy smile
            I met
            outside the café this morning.

I thought you'd like it
and would have hit send   if you
here   or   there

ii.

coffee stalls
                three dot
receipts that lead to
tight   lips   toothless
shouts   across rooms
to
laugh at (other people's) jokes
with   praise for (better) dogs

iii.

Your poem is a metaphor.
Your poem is about skinning my cheek on the sidewalk.
Your poem is not yours at all.

iv.

Strip words
like veins from a leg
or bones from a fish.

A network of movement dragged from soft tissue.

v.

There is no poem above this one.
That poem is a cactus.

As prickly as a poem.
Too dry to hit print.

vi.

The dog on the patio is a metaphor for warmth
The drool is a symbol for a pen
The coffee is a boat in a storm
The laugh is a lamp

vii.

the dog sits under the table outside
the drool is warm
the coffee: a phone call
the table is an anchor
the boat in a coffee cup
the leash is a hand
the eggshells are in the compost
the lamp is still a lamp

viii.

the dog is a means to an end
the drool is a talking point
the café is not in your neighbourhood
the coffee is an offering
the boat is unsure if it's sinking
there may or may not have been rocks
the poem is a backspace
the eggshells are in translation
the poem is a text
the dog is an olive branch
the coffee is the olive

ix.

the patio heater is broken
the leash is under the table
the drool is not like coffee
the cup is growing cold
the laugh is like the coffee cup
the message is three dots

x.

as sly as a coffee cup
the leash has come undone
the lamp won't quite turn on
the rocks are in your neighbourhood
the cheek is growing warm
the skin is not a metaphor
the laugh is on eggshells
the branch is short on olives

xi.

the three dots are a cactus
as prickly as a hair
the eggshells are in the coffee
the jokes are short on teeth
the leash snags on the olive branch
the fingertips are cold
the boat was always missing
the dog is just a dog

a greeting card

if you can't chop onions finely enough
        and reproduce via Xerox and cover tunes,
settle for describing a bitten lip
rough, damp, and threatening to split

that is to say

—floors sprout hair overnight
—grind grout down to dust
—deadhead mums
—admit they'll never live
—plan for obsolescence
—roll out another crust
—invest in clover seed
—release static in sheets
—bleach over concrete
—seal inside coats
—tug roots from their ends
—start at ground and work up
—draw all roads horizontal
—release pressure: keep safe
—paper over the cleanout
—bury heads in dust
—cough back skin cells
—retreat from the crowd
—argue for quiet
—shake twice to erase
—return shoes with scuffed toes
—set friendships in wax
—seal up doors and windows
—press hands over ears
—layer shirts and shirts
—draw circles in tight
—grow ever smaller
—lie down in the weeds
—build a fence with no gate
—stack hay bales for cats
—write over old letters
—dig basements: build down
—fasten circles of hands
—plant boots into soil
—pull apart like warm bread

—forget to be asked
—bundle up trash
—leave enough space
—consume your own lips
—cut ties with ghosts

tend

I will be a person who composts

who buys brown-spotted eggs direct from the chickens.
Who never scoops out the blood spots
    or tosses shells in the trash.
I will wash and sort my recycling.
I will bundle cardboard with rough string and gift-tie it
    in neat bows.
I will cook fresh soups from scratch.
I will wrap my leftovers in beeswax cloth softened
    against my heart.
I'll become a person who sweeps and mops the front porch
    and waves hello to the neighbours.
Who appreciates the relationship of bees to apiarist.
I will return strange mail to the sender.
I will switch from outdoor shoes to slippers.
I will become a person who can knit baby socks on
    tiny needles.
Who can tame a songbird on an outstretched hand.
I will eat crystals.
I will work miracles.
I will wake up with the sun to be mindful.
I will be a person who speaks only in song.
Who sends handwritten notes to mark minor occasions.
Who bakes crispy pies and writes in fountain pen.
I will scrawl to-do lists onto my palms.
Collect dryer lint in apron pockets.
I will be the kind of person who changes the sheets daily
    and hangs them to flutter in the cinema of the yard.
I will dream with brightness up and saturation down.
The one who consumes her receipts.
Weeds the sidewalk.
Boils the roots for tea.

buffer

1. Unroll foxes, hares, and long-tailed birds from foliage in unintrusive neutrals. Mark with pencil, pattern repeat ensuring an excess of feathers and feet.

2. Teeter on a stool with one loose leg. Fashion a plumb from a silver pendant and leftover holiday ribbon.

3. Reach crackling shoulders overhead and click. Press tacks into plaster. Warm thumbs. Hammer.

4. Join dot to dot; drop pencil. Paws swipe under door after feathers and fur.

5. Soak until sticky: collect ghosts and acorns in a cheap plastic tray.

6. Tug and shake waterlog loose. Risk splitting foxes and hares from their tails.

7. Press into shifting foundations. Trace the flight lines of squirrels. Uncover their nests.

8. Chase air pockets and clumps of fur from edges, damp blooms in reverse, cracking glue, drying feet.

9. Snap a new blade. Create only long cuts. Prune stems and flowers into neat borders. Resist overflow and rot.

10. Move strip by strip, matching hares to ears and buds to blooms.

11. Overlap flora and fauna. Dig dens under loose leaves. Seal in permanent sight lines. Buffer predators and prey.

rift

Windsor's trains demand humility // level the weight of car crashes & errands // bells catching the last bold drivers dodging falling barriers // choosing time over crush // exhale as bumpers clear // & unending cars roll on in rearview // an unbothered crawl // impervious to HR jumps & write-ups // drivers slip into park & go dark // shopping bags drag knuckles & dig grooves in hands // digital clocks tick over to late // too slow to blur the steady passing of spray paint & UP // the end must be // must be in the yard // cans of soup straining the bag // cars de- & re-coupling ahead and behind // a rift between Janette & the Tecumseh West turn // a rolling loop of trains // forward then reverse // switching tracks again while // the Bowlero crumbles // frost creeps over windows // the Moose Lodge drops letters // N T CLOS NG // infants crown & cry out // gas tanks run dry // workers retire // snowdrops bloom & fade // clouds pass overhead // soup cans split shopping bags //

any pressure can be hazardous

to disconnect:

expose skin directly to sunlight
do not protect face outdoors
       touch hot
       handles and knobs
expand capacities for risk

immerse face deep in
       applesauce, pearl barley, rhubarb
       foam, froth, and sputter
float in sensory juices

       allow rust if necessary
       seal out curvature
       protect against leakage
       hang over the edge
       for complete release.

seaming

I've been working on moving, starting at my feet
       walking in place every time my watch buzzes
       crumpling gas station receipts in my pockets
       as chunky squirrels dash across sidewalks
handfuls of garbage inch toward my knees
collar up, sealing out the wind
rubbing hives onto my throat
undercutting the chatter in the trees—
holes in each pocket   holes in armpits
                           hand-stitching
my mother cleaved its polyester seams
hiding lipsticks and change
identical in the end—bright and glossy
with permission to roam and become sand
ice and squirrels inhabiting the ends of sleeves

the other rose city

"dispatches from a bootlegging town"
kerning the rose city, no, the other one
with roses bound to Jackson Park
and thin paperback volumes,
flexing that local history muscle
but bin the line about central library
and the jab at the penis bush
scrap the lethargy of car parks:
Pacificas in idle rows
the pedestrian dignity of downtowns with no Starbucks
crack the carapace of industry, whiskey,
and slick, heavy Augusts
to anchor place to double mudds
to garlic eggplant, to injera
April thaw, tulips, and wintering fountains
insistent on the illusion
of a skyline on loan

duplex

—carve trees into my back door.
        Radio on mute, network television upstairs steaming
through the bathroom pipes, curtains, pillow covers
ash
        ceiling shakes
peat moss down through cracks in stucco
with every step rocking apt. 2's floor

        Stalactites and dust mites quake through the kitchen
            scrape the paint off cabinets
drip chilly grey water onto
breakfast dishes: soggy egg whites, coffee rings.

        Shreds of your sofa, brocade, batting and nylon
blow out through vents above my bed.

        In February,
snow melts down your steep front steps,
sneakers collecting icy runoff in our
shared lobby.
        In July, you fill my boots with sand.

innumerable shades

the webbing between my fingers
paint specks I can't scrape from floors
crawling on dusty knees from baseboard to doorframe
       good intentions to ward off cold and damp
a backpack with candy-stripe lining
a minimalist collage at an art sale
a sketch of dead rabbits in motion
shifting ductwork that leaks hot air into walls
three galvanized pots on a crumbling porch
a lost slipper through a rotten board,
       a nest for rats, raccoons, or cats
a milky crystal on a green chain
four lipstick test marks on my left thumb
discount curtains and lurid shadows
chunks of hair before my scalp wept
lower-case "love" in foil balloons
the faux-patina finish on hand-me-down forks
       never enough guests for spoons
a Pantone swatch
an imposition of succulents
the cat's tumbleweeds
a faux-fur lining
fingerprints on the fridge
blinds with teeth marks
a yoga mat with teeth marks
a sleeveless zip-up hoodie with teeth
a patch of mould on an English muffin
nails just long enough to tap on tables

tend

we tend toward moot
curl into dim mornings
set birdsong to snooze
ears plugged against purrs
press mint from a tube
a cult of warm mugs
fridge hums, bran spills
I sip, you broom

iv

other snaps

where to start

Don't start with the spine
the sunbaked transition
you begged in that
days-

                       long

                                        moment

to just
flex
please

                      dear

                                   god

just bend
or melt spray paint and scratches
into coping somehow
and tip you

                            uneventful
                            onto asphalt

before defying periodic structure
to re-form with a rough clunk and
a scrape and a heart-skip laugh
that was close, a sigh
swipe stray gravel from your thighs
indenting cellulite and razor burn
that was close to too close.

Don't start at the hip
the drop
the cartoon blue sky and *Simpsons* clouds
hair damp and catching on a flush forehead

that first-person replay
you shake roughly from your skull
in the loose minutes before sleep.

Flip over the pillow, breath catching,
and roll over from right side to left

a map of precision

in twelve
stiff movements.

stains

some stains won't rinse through—
                                        once they've had time to set.
scrub with peroxide and baking soda paste
to wrest the spots from
that mustard cropped tee, the one with the dogs
weeks dried to brown and balled
            up with jean shorts   cut
                                        through
                                        at the hip—
beg threads to let go of mascara and salt,
                creases collect sweat and grit
        reminders of that tight palm
                each line a lacuna of saline and blood.
a spill oxidized into cloth
craving wash after wash
fold three times and forget—
just to shudder the heft of cotton on skin
the clouds that passed overhead
then stalled—
                willing legs
                to split from this body
                with its nerves and its shards
                pulses that refuse
                to deaden the press of fibres and air.

july

The shivering off of translucent exteriors, less snake-like than half-life fishfly out in Belle River mid-July, shedding crisp shadows of past selves, identical castoffs on the breeze. Flick off your porch light or risk a swarm, freshly moulted masses in search of any glow. Vestigial mouths brush ears, feet grow sticky in hair, tell us *the water's growing clearer*, abandoned skins collecting in porch corners a sign of good health. In the county, they send cars fishtailing on carcasses, popping under tire treads like a firepit spitting embers that leave tiny burns in the too-long sleeves of your jumper. The shower coaxes the woodsmoke from your hair, macerates all that's between your toes, softens calluses that forget the feel of floors.

a reproduction

Choose a branch. A strong one, thick and springy. A branch fit to string as a bow, core green and supple, buoyed but not undone by tension. Raise your standards.

Skip over dry rot, wood that crunches underfoot. Slip on damp moss, kick up leaves. Stumble on loose rocks down a ravine. Don't let your feet settle.

Now draw a knife along its bark, skimming buds and fresh growth. Catch the sun through the brush. Re-pocket.

Then, with each end in a hand, begin to bend.

Past the limits of a breeze. A summer storm that bites then stills.

Pull your face tight, crease eyes against the sick pressure of too much. What your throat knows is coming: the echo, the rustle, the birds. Sap and cambium, two halves, but you don't hear the snap.

a hawk is implied risk

when you're a cat in the yard
with the nerve to paw the kitchen tile beside your bowl
the ocean whitefish and tuna dinner subpar
pushing past the gapping screen door
with grand plans of escape
from the armchair and choice of quiet nooks
that restrain you from your call
to catch&evisceration of small animals,
crickets, and those bugs that glow
taunting you nightly through the paw-marked glass,
gnawing and discarding green tomatoes in the weeds,
discounting the fleet of your claws, your needle teeth
limited to couch shredding and occasional blood

ears flicking to follow every rustle and creak
without corner cobwebs
a lone black spider to trace for hours
now just
       leaves   &
                  wires   &
                                     sky
any dark speck at risk of a swoop
some creature you've never known
but feel only as
a tingle in the scruff of your neck,
outside   just   too   open
every thermal a threat

so you,
you with the teeth
claws trimmed monthly for treats
hunker under a folding chair
jump at the twitch of a grasshopper
and plan to gut any squirrel that approaches

other snaps

Necks jut forward in a coral flounce
gladioli snap

just after blooming
    swaying gangly at the sidewalk edge
    fighting that too-tall hunch
    louder than they deserve or can stand
    you can bolster the stems with stakes
        chin up, shoulders back,
        but they tend toward fracture

    one sticky ballgown afternoon
    and then a tipping point of ants
    they pile into bathroom tissue blooms
    opportunists for flaws in natural design
    until stalks fail without echoes
    time splits seconds between upright and
    down
    and blooms shrink and wrinkle,
    shed their dry layers:
    limp and liminal
    to bury their heads in soil

corvidae

Ask me instead for my thoughts on birds forget scars for the mirror
stage of corvids unravelling contempt for crows their
       feathers in excess too loud too sharp too too
coarse to gather round shrieking in grief
oil spill and rumours
          of eyes lost to beaks

bolt

i.

The lettuce bolted. Shot to seed and tipped in the storm. Tomatoes worked through the fence, dropping green fruit, choking out the blueberry bush. What is a weed if it flowers? Draws butterflies to the window in orange and black relief? The clover hasn't quite seeded, but I root for the tiny clusters to outgrow hungry spadgers and thrive. Deadwood climbs tall as children and bursts with pink blooms. I nearly uprooted them. Some things just need time. I write the flowers down, learn their leaves and colours and names to call to the bees.

ii.

sweet woodruff for humility hewn from its temporary bed
   forget zinnia seeds until they sprout absent friends
     what's a weed but a yarrow
   thyme under grub-eaten leaves crawling for
blue salvia, I think of you until I don't
   rhododendron grows over dead cedar
     peonies too lush to be bashful
   plant a full bed of distrust, lavender for luck
ivy an invasive fidelity, married to the soil
   unassuming dill claims to guard against evil
     a folly of columbine
   a recovery of poppies

iii.

The pumpkin vine rots at its base but crawls on across pebbles:
content to open orange blossoms every morning and close again by
noon—knows it cannot sustain a gourd like the marrows that lengthen
all summer into fall. I choose a pumpkin-coloured sleeper, the size of
a fennec fox today she says or some fancy French cake or a camping
lantern.

I thumb board books about black cats and pumpkins, coo at impossibly
small and unnecessary shoes

buy a new litter box so that the cat will stop shitting on the floor.

iv.

Chopping back the rose of Sharon
tossing buds out of season to bloom in heavy piles
to dry and shrink
I sweat early fall, hacking telltale roses with Stevie Nicks on repeat
planting seeds out of season
       I don't have the triceps or the snips for thick branches that
snap rainwater across my face
      and shelter thorns with fairytale intentions.

against capital letters

an L
he repeats

not an I
but an L

forms the letter with thumb and fingers for effect

someone's hand grips a knee
my hand
someone's hand with blood drying between fingers

L is the limit
flesh is liminal
firefighters hose away what's left

L is an intersection
an affront of angles
of compound serifs
of bone

a ritual

she boils the kettle
rolling water
searches cupboards for mugs
decries our lack of proper milk
will bring her own next time, for now it's oat
and orange pekoe, family name on every box
draws a zipper bag from her purse
she brings her own tea
scorns the dregs of loose-leaf

crutches against the front window
teeth marking their grips
she tosses treats for shadows to chase
sweeps the kitchen—hangs the broom
combs hair idly through fingers, scans movie titles by row
hasn't slept right in days
hates to drive and park in the city, in the dark
won't let me wash the mugs
checks the time, checks the phone
I want to make her tea with proper milk
wash the dishes
drive her car
collect her after visiting hours
circle her in salt

origin stories for a scar

a barbed wire fence

a black bear with cubs

a dog in a hot car, a window

a midnight ritual

a weed whacker

an elevator pitch

a bear trap

an animatronic shark

a stiletto heel

a deli slicer

a mandolin

a workplace safety video

a nervous horse

an adamantium upgrade

a home ec failure

a hiding place

a landmark

a razor's glance

a jack-o-lantern's grin

a zipper

a garden

v

what remains

what remains

Crumbs, shreds of Kleenex, a damp match.
Pull off my wool socks, inside out, drag the lint from
    between my toes.
Spread peanut butter on a few crackers,
brew Earl Grey;
        rainwater rests on the windowsill
        splits flakes of wood stain,
        snails down the wall,
        books of damp faces,
        fingertip wrinkles, curls.
                Age seven, bowl cut, age nine, dinosaur t-shirt
                age eleven or twelve,
                August, perhaps June—my face was red, burnt,
                mid-afternoon by the looks of the shadows—
                I knock over my steaming mug
                thin milky brown seeps under plastic pages
                    lifts.

Greenbank

for Ivy

glass shards on pavement
a 4x4 garden with high walls
clouds gapping, so the nine o'clock sun
throws glints of Heineken green and Newcastle brown
—mosaic, but make it sharp
to keep the cats out, of course
deft paws recycling risk

we need ice cubes to expose their wounds
plastic hedgehogs and rabbits slipping
from clammy and numb hands
near losses to the front hedge
(plazzy bags and scrap card
c/o the bits-and-bobs cupboard:
PVA, Blu Tack, rubber-band balls and
pocket money for walks to Woolies)
the thrill of ultra-small-scale veterinary practice
mice and foxes perpetually *on the mend*
long let go to charity shops and the news
that the telly presenter was a predator

no one knew where the maggots went,
but the front step was buzzing

she loaned them off a fisherman by the lake
          alright, love (so she didn't push him in)

a handful of squirming bait
sprouting wings in a paper cup

the principles of woodland creatures
in green hardback books
with numbered spines that creak
"Building Now for Spring"
a heavy threat catching the breeze on a wooden stake
rubber boots and grumbles
an omen, a shiver across the backs of voles

and the rabbits, of course
blood slipping across fields
decades of dreams animating that cartoon loop
lunchtime cults and self-sacrifice
bleeding into school papers against autocracy

> *children want to see themselves in books*
> *animals have lost their draw*

but we mimed digger sabotage
dug warrens and stole real estate signs
refused meat and greeted toads
drafted alliances of adders and mice

we learned to believe
in the window cleaner
in milk in glass bottles
letters through a mail slot,
plant pots and leaded windows
the thrum of a mechanical doorbell
the daily shop in a wheelie cart
hospice for dolls with split faces
cricket in the park
spider plants hanging in pop-bottle spirals
the empty space for a jet necklace
a yellow room with drawers that jam
circuit boards and toy robots
a water heater that doesn't
the cold of the back bathroom
plastic washing tubs and Fairy liquid
the way the cooker click click clicks
the *whoosh* of gas that settles in your nose

the herb garret

in pelting sop-footed rain on the South Bank
belly warm with jackfruit and espresso
I held the rope railing and climbed stairs that were ladders
to bundles of crisp nettle and ground poppyheads
hanging over glass cases of forceps and rusty urethral sounds
dusty stuffed caimans
and floors creaking through sawdust under boards
to soak up all the blood

that must the nose remembers
returns as I trim and bundle the last of the lavender
knee straining against titanium and October damp
tie with rough twine to tug myself back to that garret
choose a suitably mouldy rafter
unencumbered with wires or bits of bikes
and wait for the luck to dry

root

i.

Some people only take root near water
tugged toward walkable riversides
that mark north or west or uptown or home.
Landlock rises in throats and draws pulses faster.
Fields and flats close like walls and traps,
but currents crack back doors.

ii.

The lurch of cars uncoupling
fog muffling horns
softens my jaw and loosens cramps:
the heavy comfort of train yards
through rain and open windows.

iii.

A railway garden over a crumbling wall
where elderflower wine takes root.
Red foxes quickstep past bedroom windows
pausing to peek in at suitcases, dolls,
damp washing steaming on rads.

iv.

The trains back home crawl,
but the ones here move like ghosts,
don't rattle the plants on the windowsill.
Did we really play on that wall,
hoisted into the railway garden,
to pause time and rescue snails?

v.

She teaches the alchemy of nettle stings
prickling across ankles
to soothe with dock leaves.
We don't have this magic back home.

vi.

Stinging nettle drives out curses,
brews tea against weakness.
I collect its sharp leaves in my side—
permanent ties to the trains, the wall
a lifelong debt of hives.

notes

"any pressure can be hazardous" uses only words that appear on the warning page of an electric pressure cooker manual.

Earlier versions of the following poems were previously published as follows:

- "origin stories for a scar" and "rerun" (as "Wild Horses") appeared in *The Puritan;*

- "thank yourself for this practice" appeared as "(practice)" in *The Dusie;*

- "any pressure can be hazardous" appeared as "Lux Model Recall" and "that is to say" appeared as "you don't say" in *periodicities;*

- "an early gift for February 14" and "duplex" appeared on the *Chaudiere Books Blog;*

- "other people's dogs" appeared in *filling Station;*

- "what remains" appeared in *The Windsor Review;*

- "a greeting card" appeared as the broadside "notes for a job interview" from above/ground press;

- "I will be a person who composts" appeared in *Vast Chasm;*

- "stains" appeared in Windsor Public Library's *Pagination;*

- "a ritual" appeared in *Contemporary Verse 2;*

- "the herb garret" and "buffer" appeared in *Janus;*

- "rift" and "the other rose city" appeared in *Words Gathered 3: Community;*

- "bolt" appeared in *Augur Magazine;*

- and "tend" appeared in *Shrapnel.*

acknowledgements

I am grateful to many people for their assistance, expertise, care, and support in the creation of this book.

Thank you to Jay and Hazel at Book*hug for giving both my poetry collections a home alongside so many wonderful titles and authors. I am truly honoured to be amongst them, and I appreciate all your work, time, and energy.

To my editor Jennifer LoveGrove for her care and insight: this manuscript changed and improved so much through our correspondence, and I am tremendously grateful. Thank you also to Gareth Lind for the gorgeous typesetting, to copy editor Andrea Waters, and to Charlene Chow for all your efforts on this book.

To my writing group that managed to pivot online during lockdown and provided much-needed motivation, inspiration, and feedback: Amilcar, Gwen, Brittni, and Theo, thank you.

To Susan and Nicole for their ongoing support of my work, including pushing me to actually write once in a while.

To Jill, Len, Stephen, and Carly for more reasons than I can count, but you already know.

To Winn and Nettle for being perfect.

And, of course, to Oliver.

about the author

Kate Hargreaves is the author of the poetry collection *Leak* as well as *Jammer Star*, a roller derby novel for young readers, and *Talking Derby*, a book of prose vignettes. She holds an MA in English and Creative Writing from the University of Windsor, where she received the Governor General's Gold Medal in Graduate Studies. Her work has appeared in literary journals across Canada, the U.S., and the U.K. As a book designer for numerous Canadian presses, Hargreaves has received honours from the Alcuin Society for Excellence in Book Design, the CBC Bookie Awards, and the Book Publishers Association of Alberta. She grew up in Amherstburg, Ontario, and lives and works in Windsor.

colophon

Manufactured as the first edition of
tend
In the fall of 2022 by Book*hug Press

Edited for the press by Jennifer LoveGrove
Copy edited by Andrea Waters
Cover by CorusKate Design
Typesetting by Gareth Lind, Lind Design
Type: CaslonCP and Mondo Serif

Printed in Canada

bookhugpress.ca